IT'S ANOTHER NEW YEAR:

Why Most New Year's Resolutions Fail, How To Set Realistic Goals

ALEJANDRO FORBES

INTRO

What will be your resolutions in the New Year? Do you plan to reinvent yourself? Or at the very least use the start of the year as a long overdue justification to break old habits or adopt new ones?

Yes, it's time to review how to keep a New Year's resolution once more. It's that time of year when we feel like we need to make a fresh start and turn over a new leaf. This is the period when we erroneously believe that the start of a New Year will miraculously bring the impetus, drive, and perseverance we need to change ourselves.

New Year's Day is customarily thought of as the perfect occasion to begin a new phase of life and the day on which you must make your crucial new year's resolution.

Being in the middle of the holiday party and vacation season, the beginning of the year is unfortunately one of the worst periods to make significant changes to your routines. This is the reason that over 85 percent of New Year's resolutions fail.

Don't set yourself up for failure by promising to make significant, difficult-to-maintain improvements. Instead, adhere to the guidelines contained in this book to successfully create New Year's resolutions that you can keep.

Table of content

Chapter One

How To Get Ready For Growth And Success In The New Year

The best moment to make a change is right now if you want to alter a behavior, or a perspective, or begin moving toward some new goals.

If you really do want to make a change, don't wait till the end of today, not next week, and not next month - start right now.

Start making any necessary changes right now. Once you've finished reading this chapter, put your book down and get active.

Dates are something that people like to give meaning to. Why not, then? It gives significance to an ordinary day. It gives us a place to start and preferably enough time to plan out what we are doing, which increases our chances of success, which leads to more success. It gives us a starting place to look at the past. It gives us a date to celebrate. When we achieve them, it gives our successes meaning and purpose.

We, therefore, go through the process of choosing "New Year's resolutions" and preparing (or not really) for changes that we wish to make every year around December and January.

Many of these goals are not achieved or are quickly forgotten. You may set yourself up for greater self-growth and increase your chances of sticking to your resolutions in the New Year—or really, whenever you want to start the process of change—by following the advice contained in this chapter and subsequent chapters.

In this chapter, a three-step process is outlined on how you can achieve whatever is your goal in the New Year. The three-step process is a great approach to start the New Year off right and get ready for growth.

However, beware - it's not as simple as "state your objectives and makes a plan.

For the goals for change we set for ourselves to be meaningful and applicable, it requires some deeper introspection.

First Step: *Cast your mind back to your previous year, review it*

For new growth, this phase is critical. We frequently ignore it and set goals or pursue changes that don't necessarily correspond to where we are and where we genuinely want to be.

Look back on the previous year and your successes and mistakes.

What did and did not work for you?

What did you do to make your triumphs possible?

How else did you add to your flaws?

This will provide you some food for thought for what happens next, how to steer your ship and advice on what to repeat and what not to repeat.

Then consider your feelings towards your accomplishments and shortcomings. No, really—what are your opinions and sentiments on whether or not anything was accomplished?

This is an essential component that must not be overlooked because our thoughts and feelings control our behavior.

Is there anything left undone, unfinished, or unattended? This includes any unclaimed rewards for your victories and plans to make up for any shortcomings.

Recognize both the positive and negative. If you haven't already, pat yourself on the back when it's due, but also take lessons from the things that didn't go your way. Without a lesson, a tragic incident is merely a waste of time. A valuable resource we can never get back is time.

Ask yourself, "What can I change? What do I need to change? What are the underlying problems that have motivated me to look for growth and change?

Although we haven't yet defined our new objectives, we are beginning to at least present some thoughts.

Step Two: *Rebuild*

Although the rebuilding phase has many difficult aspects, it also gives us the chance to heal and get ready for our adventure. Here, apologies, amends, and forgiveness all take place.

We leave unfinished business and duties if we don't think these things out. Those can resurface and become obstacles to our development and prosperity.

Do you feel the need to "make it right" or owe anyone an apology, including yourself?

Do it as long as you won't be causing further suffering or difficulties.

How can I forget my mistakes and those of others? Even while it is important for progress, this is not as easily addressed, particularly when it comes to forgiving oneself.

Consider your reflection phase's shortcomings or strengths. How do you perceive them? Refine your understanding of what things mean to you and, if necessary, modify your way of thinking.

Finding the "silver lining" in a less-than-ideal situation or learning a lesson from a tragic occurrence is equivalent to doing this. You will be in a better position to develop if you view these setbacks as only a brief slip backward or bump in the road that you learned from, as opposed to an absolute failure.

Finally, consider how you can better yourself to reduce future conflicts and misunderstandings.

Third Step: *Revitalize*

Here, we lay the groundwork and plan for our future development. Although the phases that came before were essential, if we don't properly stimulate ourselves, we will become stagnant. You wouldn't go out on a road trip with the gas gauge at 'E', would you?

Find your purpose.

What spurs you on and drives you? Why do you require this development or change? What do they mean to you specifically? How do I matter or fit into the bigger picture?

In addition to pushing you and keeping you on the path of personal development, the answers to these questions will serve as a compass for your journey.

To assist you to have your plate as clear as possible for the New Year, take care of any little issues or tasks. You'll feel fantastic when you complete even the smallest tasks in advance of your significant shift.

Create your change-related plans and enlist support. Now that you have completed all of your self-evaluations, it is time to set your goals.

Connect your objectives to your planned development, change, and "why."

Make sure your formal goals are Smart Time-based, Relevant, Specific, Measurable, and Achievable
when you define them.

Decide next where you can use assistance and who can help you with your growth strategy. You are not by yourself.

When we use assistance and encouragement, even if it means accepting a large slice of a humble pie, we boost our chances of success.

Set goals for yourself and decide how you will reward yourself along the way. We must prepare for doing it ourselves because we don't always receive credit or compensation.

Imagine yourself carrying out your plan and imagining what it will be like to achieve your goals. even imagine flaws. This will help you get ready for any unforeseen circumstances that could affect your plan.

You now have it. The challenging path to achievement and progress in the coming year. Even though change is a stressful process, managing it well and making proper preparations will help to lessen the stress we put ourselves through.

You've just read the chapter. You can now put the book down for some minutes and get active.

Chapter Two

Make A Difference. Don't End The New Year With Regrets

It's possible to make resolutions and keep to them. But that is if you are determined.

If you want your resolutions to be part of the few success stories, take note of the following:

When you review the past year list your accomplishments

Before beginning a new year, looking back on the previous one is a terrific method to determine the aspects of your life that are "on point" so you can recognize your successes. As another new year beckons, your sense of success will be at its height, giving you the confidence to accomplish everything you set your mind to.

Create a vision map

You can use a visual map as a practical tool to help you stay committed to and complete your goals throughout the future year. All you need to make is a pen and four sheets of paper. Write your goals for the appropriate quarter on each page, along with any observations you have from the previous year that will help you achieve your goals.

This visual plan will be helpful to keep in mind during the new year so that you may have a clear idea of what you will be doing.

Examine your routines

This may need some introspection on your part but will be very helpful to you.

Examining all of your habits—yes, including the negative ones—can help you decide what behaviors you want to adopt in the next year. You'll want your behaviors to align with the level of achievement you want. Make a note of the areas that require improvement and devise a strategy for doing so while forming new habits.

Alter your environment

Your environment has a significant impact on your general thinking, which is one of the most important factors in success. In fact, according to Psychology Today, rearranging your environment can directly affect your mood and give you a sense of efficacy. Even a small gesture, like placing fresh flowers on your desk once a week, may keep your spirits up and inspire you to succeed every day.

Establish a wellness schedule

Above all things, you must look after yourself if you want to succeed. A wellness regimen will give you the guidelines for taking care of your most valuable asset, You, in the new year. Exercise, drinking enough water, receiving a massage once a month, taking care of your skin every day, and frequent visits to your favorite coffee shop are all components of a health routine that should be scheduled into your schedule for the New Year.

No matter what your situation, you can make the New Year fantastic for yourself if you're willing and determined to take control of your life and finally stand up for yourself!

What actions (new or old) are you planning to do in the New Year?

Select One Item

Don't attempt to alter every aspect of your life or way of living at once if you want to make changes. It will fail. Choose one aspect of your life to start changing instead.

Making a real commitment that you can follow through on will help you know exactly what changes you're trying to make.

After a month or so, if the first adjustment is a success, you can move on to the next one. You still have the option to be a whole new you at the end of the year by making modest adjustments one at a time, and this is a far more practical approach.

Don't choose a New Year's resolution that you know will fail, such as running a marathon if you weigh 42 pounds too much and have trouble breathing when climbing stairs

If that's the case, decide to set goals for the new year that will inspire you to go for daily walks. Perhaps this will help you lose weight.

Once you've mastered that habit, you can advance to running in short bursts, continuous running by March or April, and a marathon after the year. Which habit do you wish to modify the most?

Make a plan

Making resolutions for the new year is no easy task. It's even tougher to learn how to keep resolutions.

Do not wait until the last minute if you want to succeed. To ensure you have the resources you need when you need them, you should investigate the change you're making and make a strategy.

Here are some things you can do to get ready and set up all the necessary systems for your change.

Learn more about it by getting books on the topic from the library. There are publications to help you get ready for any change, whether it be giving up smoking, starting a jogging or yoga practice, or going vegan. either that or go online.

Make each moment of your life matter!

If you do sufficient research and dedicate enough effort to your resolutions, you will eagerly anticipate making the change.

Create a plan for success and get everything ready to ensure a smooth process. If you decide to start running, be sure to have your sneakers, outfit, hat, sunglasses, and iPod ready with some upbeat music.

You could even find a partner to work with. Working alongside a buddy or coworker can help you make better decisions.

There are no valid defenses. One of the reasons resolves fail is due to this.

Prepare for issues

Your aim will not be simple to achieve. Make a list of the issues that will arise since there will be issues. If you give it some thought, you'll be able to foresee issues during particular times of the day, with particular individuals, or in particular circumstances.

Work out strategies to deal with them when they inevitably arise once you've identified the periods that will likely be difficult. You can learn how to keep new year's resolutions if you keep this advice in mind.

Monitor your development

Nothing inspires you more than realizing how far you've come. Tracking your progress will help you feel more confident that you are moving on the correct path. This is now simple to achieve because of technology.

For instance, you could use an app to mark the days that you made progress toward your objective. You can also develop a spreadsheet that will help you visualize your progress if you want to go the extra mile.

You'll be more driven to continue on the right path once you see how far you've come and how well all of your sacrifices paid off. For days when you feel like your motivation is waning, reviewing all the effort you have put in is a great tactic.

Consider your previous mistakes

As stated earlier, it is important to take a look at your past failures. This is one of the best resolution-making tips you will ever discover. You won't make those errors again if you do it this way.

Your self-esteem will suffer greatly if you keep making the same errors year after year.

Consider your prior lapses if you want to make new year's resolutions that you won't keep. What decisions did you make that allowed you to escape it? Did anything inspire you to put forth more effort toward accomplishing your goal?

Be as adaptable as you possibly can. There is nothing wrong with changing your goal to something more achievable. Who knows, if you switch up your strategy, you might have better outcomes.

Try it out

Go all out on your big day. Commit and record it on a card when learning how to make a new year's resolution.

All you need is a single, compact phrase that you can keep in your wallet. Keep it near your bed, in your car, and on your bathroom mirror for an additional boost in motivation.

Chapter Three

Learn From Successful People

Many people who aspire to success believe that success occurs by accident and lose sight of the truth that achieving goals requires personal consistency and perseverance.

Success is more dependent on regularity than random events.

There is no single, obvious route to success. Success comes to various people in different ways, but there are several characteristics that successful people share that enable them to accomplish their objectives.

It's critical to understand the qualities you need and how to develop them if you want to succeed in whatever you set your mind on achieving in life.

Here are a few practices that successful people have used to attain their objectives:

They put up a lot of effort

Michael Jordan once said, "I always thought that if you put in the work, success will come.

If you want to succeed, you must concentrate on the effort that will lead to your success. Before you succeed, you must put in the time and work. You can get into too many areas you otherwise wouldn't be able to with persistence, discipline, and a desire to work hard.

They prepare

Journaling helps people to stay on track with their goals and remember their progress. You need a plan that will motivate you to keep moving forward and show you how to get where you're going.

They act and don't put things off

Without action, thinking and dreaming have no real purpose. Successful people have developed the habit of acting. Even when they don't feel completely ready or emotionally prepared, they occasionally act bravely.

They have certain objectives

They concentrate on getting to where they want to be. They don't procrastinate or try to chase several things at once. No, they put their attention on objectives that they are confident can be reached in a reasonable amount of time. They are inspired to develop the mental toughness needed to attain their goal through this rigorous technique.

They devour books

Not everyone who reads extensively is a leader. A reader, however, is a leader. If you don't study or take the time to learn, you won't be able to achieve your goals. Successful people have the habit of reading, which broadens their horizons. They are also aware of the value of learning from the experiences of others to advance one's knowledge.

Every successful person has a strong passion for their particular ability, profession, or craft. They don't merely do it for the cash. Instead, they do it out of a passion for it and the pleasure it brings them. As a result, they make sure that their daily routines are focused on things that will bring out the best in them and, in doing so, get them closer to success.

Self-assurance

Another characteristic of those who succeed in their goals is self-assurance. You must first believe in your abilities if you want to succeed in anything. Having this self-assurance enables you to pursue your goals and persevere through your efforts.

Drive

Drive entails motivation and initiative. It inspires those poised for success to achieve their objectives, this is one of the essential characteristics of successful people. Although having objectives is crucial, the ability to turn those aspirations into reality depends on a person's desire.

Self-control

Discipline is a quality shared by successful people together with desire and perseverance. Once they are inspired to do anything, they put in a lot of effort and perseverance to get it done. People that have a high work ethic are more successful. If you have discipline, you can create routines and habits that help you succeed.

Positivity

The ability to maintain optimism despite difficulties is a trait of successful people. This is not to say that you shouldn't or can't be realistic. Imagining your achievement can be a crucial step in making it a reality, thus optimism is a valuable quality to possess.

Feeling

You can achieve your goals if you are passionate about what you do. You have to care about something deeply to work for it. Similar to how important drive is, passion motivates you to put in more effort to accomplish your goals.

However, whereas passion focuses on the path to success and how to make the process more joyful, the drive is more about the final goal and the will to get there.

Fortitude

Resilience is the final quality that successful individuals possess. It may not always be possible to succeed right away or on your first attempt, therefore it's critical to maintain your perseverance.

When faced with setbacks or difficulties, resilience enables you to endure and try again until you are successful.

This is among the qualities that are most crucial for success since it prevents people from giving up on their ambitions.

Chapter Four

Most New Year's Resolutions Fail And Here Are The Whys

You might not need to look far to identify those whose past New Year's resolutions never amount to anything as you might be a typical example of one of them.

If you are one of those, you are not alone, the majority of people don't even realize their New Year's resolutions. If you want to be among the few who achieve theirs or at least get very close to it, this chapter will assist you.

Know that an entirely fresh chapter beginning in the book of your life is eloquently represented by a new year. But while so many individuals strive to meet lofty objectives, only a few individuals will ever taste success.

Most people abandon their New Year's resolutions soon after making them and the reason why they do so is explained in this chapter.

Why do New Year's resolutions fail? Here are some of the major reasons:

Treating a marathon like a sprint

No one sets out at full speed in a marathon without crashing sooner than later. You dare not treat a marathon as a sprint.

The mistake many people make in their New Year's resolutions is the "I want it all and I want it now" syndrome.

The mentality of wanting it all and wanting it now is much less effective than gradual habit change. It may not be hot, but it's a lot more effective.

Because they aren't overwhelming, small changes are more likely to persist. If done correctly, you may not even notice them.

It's not necessary to completely overhaul your life overnight if you currently have a lot of unhealthy habits. You want to get thinner. Stop the extreme fitness programs and crash diets!

The reason why so many New Year's resolutions and other goals fail is that people don't take intentional, exact action.

Add one wholesome habit per week as opposed to adhering to a very tight schedule that forbids all enjoyment. For instance, during your first week, you could start by consuming more water.

You might progress to consuming three fruits and vegetables each day the following week. A fistful of protein could be consumed at each meal over the following week.

Placing the cart before the horse

Don't even consider supplementing a poor diet since it's dumb. Pay close attention to the activities that yield the most fruitful outcomes. Avoid worrying over anything if it is unimportant.

Lack self-confidence

Before you ever get off the ground, inaction can cripple you. It could be difficult to have faith in yourself if you've previously tried and failed to make a New Year's Resolution. Your inner critic, and doubt, will fight tooth and nail to prevent you from moving forward in your life.

Only by having faith in oneself can doubt be overcome. Why should anyone care if you've made mistakes before? You can try one more this year, but better this time.

Thinking too much rather than acting

If you don't act, no amount of self-help literature will be able to save you.

As a Chinese Proverb says,
"The best time to plant a tree was 20 years ago. The second best time is now."

Inspire yourself and learn as much as you can, but only to the extent that it will benefit your life. You'll be well on your way to success if you can use even one item you learn from each book or article you read.

You're in way too much of a rush

It is in your best interest to practice patience since everyone would do it if it were quick and simple.

You are not enjoying the process

When people view eating as a duty and exercise as a painful bore, is it any wonder that they struggle with their weight?

A fitness program that disrupts your everyday routine the least is the greatest one. The objective is to reduce your stress levels, not increase them.

Make exercising pleasurable, however, you have to do it since even the greatest among us can't force ourselves to do something we detest constantly.

This may involve taking part in a sport you enjoy, working out with a friend or two, signing up for a group fitness class so you can meet new people, or allowing yourself one "free day" each week to forgo your training schedule and exercise any way you choose.

You struggle too much

Avoid depriving your body of pleasure unless you want to develop unpleasant urges. You'll crave food more if you deprive yourself of it more often.

The easier approach is to embrace a 12-month plan where you're making regular changes, rather than trying to overhaul every aspect of your life in one month.

Don't worry about the occasional indulgence if you're making good decisions 80–90 percent of the time.

You don't monitor your development

It will be easier for you to maintain an "I can do this" attitude if you keep a written log of your training progress. A notebook and a pen are all you need.

Keep track of the exercises you execute, the number of repetitions you complete, and the weight you used, if any, for each workout. Your aim? Don't repeat that mistake.

Regularly improving your best performance provides you with encouraging feedback that will motivate you to keep going.

You don't have social support

When you feel isolated, it can be challenging to maintain motivation. The positive news - is far from being alone, you are not. Ask your social media friends if anyone would want to be your workout or accountability buddy in a status update.

Try to schedule your lunch hour and go out together if you know a coworker who shares your aim so that you'll be more likely to make wise choices.

The numbers are not on your side

Only about nine percent of those who make resolutions for the new year can keep them, according to research.

Although both success and failure are a part of life, are these numbers actually motivating?

Consider the case when you choose to make a New Year's Resolution and are an upbeat individual. What would happen if you were among the 92 percent of the unsuccessful people? What would happen if your wise goals or resolutions were to succeed every year, too?

With the above statistics, it seems like making a New Year goal is just setting yourself up for failure.

Contrary results from New Year resolutions are rare. If you are among those who have attempted to keep New Year's resolutions in the past but failed, you can probably connect to this reality. Many people make resolutions to stop smoking, eat less, get up earlier, exercise more, etc.

But as time goes on, people's will to stay the course wanes and they revert to their former routines.

The saddest aspect is that they have lost even more of their ability to maintain their resolution! People often smoke more when they start smoking again after an unsuccessful attempt at a New Year's goal for instance, and the same is true of other types of resolutions.

Just consider it now! People revert to their previous habits of eating junk food instead of making healthier dietary choices!

Isn't it unfortunate that people who once smoked five cigarettes a day now smoke more than ten?

These efforts just serve to exacerbate the situation!

Creating and breaking habits is a lifelong task. Any task that involves quitting smoking, regular exercise, or weight management cannot be completed in a single day. If you wish to achieve these goals, you must be consistent. something that is not time-based.

Isn't it true that when you make a New Year's goal to give up smoking, you don't simply mean to do it for a day or two but for good? It is a behavior and a method that will help you succeed. Resolving won't help you achieve your goals; only your determination will!

You're just putting it off.
Why wait for a certain date if you genuinely want to do it?

Some people even think that making New Year's resolutions is just a copy-and-paste trick! Confused? People copy the resolve of others they find fascinating or difficult, much like one can copy the text in a word document!

Why wait for a specific date if something is so important to you? That is the question. Your objectives, both short-term and long-term, are not time-bound.

Why torture your body with excessive intake until some fictitious resolve date, whether it's giving up booze or losing weight? Do you want to stick to your desire for junk food, drink, or smoking for a few days more? Make your resolution now and start the process to end it.

Don't you think it's true that most people who make New Year's resolutions quickly revert to their previous routines?

The takeaway is that you don't need to wait for a specific day to begin making an effort if you truly want to do something or give something up. Your future's shaping events start right now!

Lack of success brings negativity

People who break their resolutions frequently feel bad about choosing the first place. They provide explanations for their mistakes or even assign blame. Anger and negativity are reflected in the behavior that follows.

Every year, almost 90 percent of resolutions are broken.

Imagine what might transpire if the same event kept happening. Would you be beaming with self-assurance or second-guessing your choices?

All the courage and hard work that went into making those resolutions were for naught. Eventually, pessimism takes the place of audacity in your mind, trapping you into thinking that you cannot carry out your resolution.

You are aware of what you are, but not why

The main cause of most New Year resolutions' failure is that most people know what they want but don't understand why they want it.

Yes, you want to be healthy, fit or lose weight. But why is your objective so crucial to you? For instance:

Do you want to be healthy so that you can set a good example for your kids to follow?

Do you want to reduce weight to feel sexier and more self-assured about your physique than ever before?

Do you desire good health so that you can live more clearly, energetically, and purposefully in all facets of your life?

It's up to you whether you want to live longer, set a good example, have more energy, feel more confident, have a reason to buy stylish new clothes, or improve your chances of finding love. (I'm not a judge anyway.

However, be loyal to yourself and set aside any preconceptions.

It is more likely that you will succeed if you can make your goal as specific as you can. This will make it more vivid in your mind.

Why do most of us establish plans with such fervor and purpose but then fail to carry them out? Do we lack self-assurance or motivation? Or might it be a lack of willpower?

Whatever the cause, it undoubtedly prompts us to consider whether our entire New Year's Resolution is a horrible idea.

People make resolutions for the New Year to stop drinking, get in shape, kick bad habits, etc. Few people, however, are aware of the long-term consequences of breaking New Year's resolutions.

So, don't wait till the new year if you genuinely want to accomplish a goal. Simply reflect on why you're doing it and begin to prepare for it.

Chapter Five

How It Will End - Success Or Failure - It's Your Choice

Failure and success are decisions, and by making some minor adjustments to your perspective and attitude, you may stay off the path that leads to nothing but sorrow.

You're on the road to success if you don't let any negative emotions, like frustration, make you feel helpless, insignificant, or weak.

Refocus and realign yourself, and if you don't already have a goal or vision for your life, make one now. This is your life, and you should enjoy it and make the most of it.

Make Your choice. You only get one life. Life is a single opportunity. That is all we have.

What would be the most courageous version of me today? This is the question you should ask yourself. Find your answer, then carry it out. You won't regret doing it!

Decide to lead a rich, complete, and fulfilling life. A successful existence.
If you need a boost, perhaps this article will motivate you to take action.

Remember, failure is never a certainty; so is success.

It's possible to fail at anything. When individuals say it's not, what they mean is that they won't allow themselves to choose failure.

No one ever chooses to be a failure in any endeavor. Who decides to lose?

Whether we are aware of it or not, a lot of the decisions we make every day affect the outcomes of our efforts, even if we frequently fail to notice the connection between these decisions and our chances of success.

Our finest efforts can be thwarted by four small decisions that make failure a real possibility:

a. Not practicing restraint

Everybody struggles from time to time with self-control in some area of their lives. Everybody's version of it is different, but the inability to maintain equilibrium is harmful and can cost us a lot if we don't address it.

Any number of things, including eating, relationship boundaries, sex, or gambling, as well as swearing, chocolate, rage, smoking, or even exercise, can be a source of struggle.

I know a friend whose video games were his vice when he first started in a company. He would purchase the newest game and play all night. He would then leave for work, produce little, and return the following evening to continue playing until he won the game.

Later, he understood the need of tracking his time usage. He plotted out his typical day in 30-minute chunks to see how he was using his time, and he was shocked to see that he was wasting more time on games than he was working on his business. At this point, he had to decide between succeeding in his business or succeeding in late-night video gaming. He went with option one.

If you want to succeed at anything, avoid letting a lack of self-control cause you to fail since it is always possible. Determine success.

b. *Believing you can handle it by yourself*

We tend to believe that we must do it alone when we are working hard. This mentality, which has the potential to be harmful and destructive, is particularly vulnerable in men. We are wired to work together, as evidenced by every aspect of our biology. Even something as basic as a hug sends feel-good chemicals to our brains, demonstrating the need and desire for connection.

Learn to build a strong support network as it will help you to achieve your goals and dreams easier.

Avoid going it alone. Failure is a possibility for you if you believe you can.

Every man is a part of the globe, not an island, and no one exists in isolation.

c. *Deciding to withdraw*

We all require solitude. That is not the issue we are looking at. but those times when things are difficult and nothing seems to be going well. We tend to shrink and run away from people and situations at this time.

Be especially self-aware during difficult times because when we withdraw to hide, failure is an option. We don't always recognize when we are hiding in our TV, hobbies, excessive sleep, etc.

d. *Believing you are an expert*

Keep an open mind and a learning attitude. Things that first operate well can later need to be reevaluated. New autos ultimately develop problems.

When the environment they are in changes, successful routines become unsustainable. New methods of reaching customers also arise as business trends evolve. Failure is not merely a possibility if you are unwilling to change and grow.

Every decision we make has an impact. It's possible to fail at anything, as it is possible to succeed at anything.

Chapter Six

Incredible Facts About New Year's Resolutions You Should Know

resolutions for the New Year have been made since the Babylonians celebrated their first barley harvest 4,000 years ago.

They didn't make the resolutions on January 1st, but in the middle of March, when they had a 12-day festival called Akitu to commemorate the spring barley crop.

But about 38.5 percent of US individuals still make resolutions each year, indicating that these practices are still common in modern society. Exercise more, eating healthier, and losing weight are the three most common health-related goals.

Unfortunately, research has shown that 23 percent of people fail in the first week, and 43 percent anticipate failing before February. The timing of New Year's resolutions appears to be the key factor, as many aren't yet prepared to commit.

What is the key to joining about nine percent of people that succeed? Only make resolutions for the new year that are timely, particular to you, and relevant.

Success is determined by two factors.

Acquiring knowledge in your area of interest and the skills necessary to reach self-mastery is the first step.

Second, your capacity for putting that knowledge to use and developing wisdom.

This book is entirely meant to assist you to master those skills and live a more fulfilling life without giving up pleasure.

With what you have learned so far, you are not expected to make New Year's resolutions and fail to succeed.

For emphasis' sake, remember that millions of people make New Year's resolutions each year, and many of them fail to keep them after the first week.

How successful are New Year's resolutions, then?

What distinguishes those who set goals and achieve them from everyone else?

It is important you know this so that you can make up your mind.

The timing of New Year's resolutions is the key factor in failure. While there is a desire for change, many are not yet prepared to fully commit.

More successful people said they had more stimuli control and willpower. After the first six months of working toward the objective, interpersonal skills and social support become crucial.

Successful people commonly make 14-15 mistakes over two years, which suggests that resilience—the capacity to recover from setbacks—is crucial for achieving goals.

As earlier stated, the ideal time to begin is anytime you are prepared to commit to your goals. In other words, pick the New Year's resolutions that are the most pertinent and urgent.

Make the aim lower if you want to keep a New Year's resolution but feel unprepared to do so. For instance, start with altering what you eat for breakfast rather than making a vow to modify your entire diet.

Chapter Seven

Resolutions For The New Year That Are Bound To Fail

From research, the following resolutions appear to be among the worst ones to make. They're probably going to fail. Aside from pointing out these worst resolutions, this book also reveals what you can do to make sure you overcome them.

Start a January diet resolution

One of the most popular resolutions for the new year is to start a diet, so it makes sense that many people fail at it.

The gloomy depths of winter will certainly overcome willpower if the leftover mince pies and chocolates aren't enough to do so. Depriving yourself during the coldest months will only result in further heartbreak.

If your goal is to lose weight, choose the best time to start and get ready for it beforehand. Make sure to plan healthy meals, stay away from fad diets, find a jogging partner, and, most importantly, finish all the mince pies.

Sign up for a gym resolution

For those looking to get fit and healthy after the holiday season, joining a gym is a popular option alongside dieting.

You don't need to pay for a costly gym membership or force yourself to leave the house to improve your health and fitness, which makes up 51 percent of New Year's plans made in Britain.

Without ever setting foot inside the dreaded gym, you may get fit and healthy by creating your training regimen using commonplace objects like food tins and water bottles.

Leave the country resolution

If you only receive two weeks of employment a year and two of them are already booked up with dentist appointments and Grandma's birthday dinner, choosing to travel more is likely to result in disappointment.

If it turns out that the year is not right for a global excursion, many intriguing places in some countries of the world are worth a trip and offer a plethora of outdoor activities and cultural experiences for a fraction of the time and expense of traveling around the world.

Organize my life resolution

It's a good start if you're organized enough to desire to organize yourself.

If the work is too big, you're more likely to fail to get things in order, so make lists of everything you want to organize and then break those lists down further into smaller objectives.

This method is effective for organizing everything you want, including your finances or travel arrangements.

Enjoy life resolution

Resolving to be content for an entire year is a difficult, if not impossible endeavor.

Instead, push yourself to adopt a more optimistic mindset.

Positive thinking increases longevity, lowers stress levels, and fosters both physical and mental health.

Spend less money resolution

The problem is that it feels like every day is "rainy," thus being thrifty and saving money for a rainy day is a popular resolution made at the beginning of the year.

A growing number of people are being tempted to use their money to increase their level of happiness in the face of depressing weather, an unsteady economy, and uncertain political prospects.

Saving money isn't the most fun thing in the world, but if you can keep at it, you might own that new car, trip, or house by the end of the year.

Consider a new career resolution

Are you considering changing careers this year? You're not alone; as a resolution, many people plan to pursue a new job goal.

Before using this strategy, you should ask yourself several questions, such as: Is it realistic for you to take the risk? Do you believe the grass will be greener?

In any case, it is not advised to think about this at the stroke of midnight when the celebration is in full flow. You don't want to have a headache in January and no work to return to.

Get my ex-back resolution

We've all been fixated on that one breakup for the past few months, and we all regret it.

Or how about the elusive one? But not every lost love merits a second chance.

Why spend an entire year on something that is most likely not going to occur? After all, there are lots of other fish.

How to keep your resolutions from the previous year:

- Be truthful
- Enlist the help of family and friends
- Take manageable incremental steps
- Gratify yourself
- Adapt from any failures
- Make permanent habit changes

Don't set yourself up for failure whether you're making resolutions for the fiftieth time or aiming to make changes for the first time.

Take advantage of the new year and the new you by following the advice contained in this book for success.

www.ingramcontent.com/pod-product-compliance
Lightning Source LLC
LaVergne TN
LVHW050342160826
845677LV00014B/3739

* 9 7 9 8 3 6 7 8 0 3 3 4 1 *